Pauline Ball

Maths Activities for Infants

$$\begin{array}{r} 52 \\ +\ 46 \\ \hline 98 \end{array}$$

CAMBRIDGE
UNIVERSITY PRESS

Published by the Press Syndicate of the University of Cambridge
The Pitt Building, Trumpington Street, Cambridge CB2 1RP
40 West 20th Street, New York, NY 10011-4211, USA
10 Stamford Road, Oakleigh, Victoria 3166, Australia

© Cambridge University Press 1992

First published 1992

Printed in Great Britain

A catalogue record for this book is available from the British Library

Cartoon illustrations by Harry Venning
Cover illustration by Emma Whiting

ISBN 0 521 43967 1

Contents

Introduction

This book contains a wide variety of mathematics activities covering most of the National Curriculum in Mathematics for the later stages of Key Stage 1. Many of the activities are appropriate at levels 1 and 2, offering alternative approaches or extensions to enable children to develop through level 3 and sometimes further.

As the National Curriculum document changes through revisions and re-writings, precise referencing proves difficult. However, these activities are referenced to the latest publication *Mathematics in the National Curriculum* (1991).

All the activities suggested here have been tried and tested in infant classrooms, and most use only the most basic normal classroom equipment. Each activity is preceded by a brief list of equipment required, and several activities offer suggestions for extensions, perhaps with a variation of equipment. Activities which include the use of a calculator are shown with a calculator symbol in the margin.

calculator

small group

large group

The aim has been to suggest a variety of shorter and longer activities, some for use with whole classes and some for smaller groups, some for specific teaching, and some with incidental learning opportunities embodied within the activities. Those most appropriate to small group or large group work are accompanied by that symbol in the margin. Some of the activities are very specific, some are more general, offering opportunities for extensions to a higher level, or to a different aspect of the mathematics curriculum. Many of the activities

science

are cross-curricular, or offer opportunities for cross-curricular links, reflecting the way in which mathematics permeates all aspects of school and of life. Activities with strong ties in other subjects are accompanied by the appropriate symbol in the margin.

art

While specifically written for the purposes of teaching and learning, many of these activities can be adapted for the purposes of teacher assessment, sometimes with only a simple alteration of context or apparatus, enabling children to show what they have learnt from an activity, and to generalise their learning into areas other than those specifically taught.

geography

Activities have been arranged approximately in an order dictated by the National Curriculum document. Variations occur where the nature of the activities, or the quantity of material demanded by the Attainment Target, so dictate. The reference in the margin indicates the main AT and level related to the activity. Many of the activities provide opportunities for learning within other ATs, which has not necessarily been noted.

PE

design
and
technology

Mathematics in the Classroom

An infants' classroom which is well set up for effective mathematical learning will always contain a wide selection of equipment, attractively displayed, and freely accessible to children. Much of the equipment needed can be collected, or will be in the classroom for other purposes. In some instances it is possible to make your own or substitute. But it is essential that children become accustomed to using a variety of equipment to enable them to select and to generalise.

This is a suggested list. It is not exhaustive, and other items will be equally acceptable, but it offers a guide to what should be available to children.

- marbles
- conkers
- pine cones
- dried peas
- stones
- linking cubes
- buttons
- weights
- balancing scales
- kitchen-type scales
- tape measures
- rulers
  - short (20 or 30 cm)
  - long (1 m)
- 2D shapes
- 3D shapes
- junk boxes

- parcels of various sizes and weights
- 6-sided dice
  - marked with numbers
  - marked with spots
- multisided dice
- coins
- a working clock
- clock faces
- sorting tray
- calculators
- pegs and pegboard
- pinboard and rubber bands
- sand tray
- water tray
- volume and capacity containers

- timetable of the week
- calendar with significant dates marked
- crockery and cutlery in the home corner
- a shop for free play and more structured work
- 2 cm squared paper
- a number line to 100, which starts before 0
- lengths of string, wool or ribbon
- a selection of simple board games
- 1-minute and 3-minute timers
- stop clock

Using and Applying Mathematics

Mathematics is to be found all around us, in almost everything we do. We should take every possible opportunity to point out the mathematics in everyday situations, to help children to see the uses and applications of mathematics, and to develop classroom skills directly from real life. In this way the subject will be seen not as strange, difficult or threatening, but as a natural part of our lives and as a powerful tool which can help us to explain many things which would otherwise carry less meaning.

AT 1

'Using and applying mathematics' implies a complete approach to a way of working. It involves children thinking about and questioning what they are doing, and takes mathematical learning through and beyond traditional methods of teaching computation. As children progress through the first Attainment Target of the National Curriculum, they will develop and demonstrate a confidence in, and a competence with, mathematical tasks which cannot be encouraged through purely rote methods of learning.

AT 1:1a

Children using the sand or water tray are developing the mathematical concepts of measurement, weight and volume. Construction apparatus provides endless opportunities for exploring spatial concepts, counting,

7

3D shape, sorting and the early stages of the properties of different shapes. A well-equipped home corner provides experience of one-to-one correspondence, counting, matching and sorting; cooking offers scope for estimating, weighing and timing, and the class shop is an ideal setting for handling and beginning to understand money. Making models increases experience with size, dimension and 3D shapes, and leads, through discussion, to vocabulary such as 'taller', 'longer', 'wider', 'more than' and other similar language.

AT 1:1b

AT 1:1c

Free classroom use of objects to count, measure and weigh or balance can provide the experience which will enable children to reason and predict when asked relevant questions. Provision of a range of parcels of different sizes and weights and other objects, such as stones, pine cones or marbles can encourage incidental learning, as well as their being available for planned teaching. Children who have free access to, and use, these sorts of apparatus will gain the experience they need on which they can base predictions and develop a questioning mind.

AT 1:2a

An open display of mathematics apparatus will encourage children to select the materials and the mathematics they need for a practical task. Such selection can be developed by encouraging discussion between the children of a task set, and by asking for suggestions of what they think would be appropriate from the very beginning. They will quickly understand and adopt your thinking and reasoning for particular apparatus or methods, and begin naturally to use similar reasoning themselves.

From the very earliest, unstructured mathematics in the classroom, and through all the structured teaching and learning, children need encouragement to talk about the

AT 1: 2b

mathematics they are using. Talking, discussing and explaining their thinking and calculations will help them to understand more clearly, and often help them to spot and correct their own mistakes (making similar mistakes less likely another time). Encouraging children to ask questions about what they are learning develops an open approach to mathematics and a healthy awareness that asking questions and having them answered can help them to understand and enjoy their work.

AT 1: 2c

We can develop childrens' confidence in mathematics by asking them to respond to questions such as 'Why?' or 'Are you sure?', particularly when their reasoning is correct, as this helps them to verbalise their learning or assumptions. Such questions also quickly reveal children who have 'guessed' and whose learning is not complete. The value of open-ended questioning in mathematics cannot be over-emphasised. Children readily pick up clues from teachers about the accuracy of their answer to a closed question, and can too easily develop a concern about the 'wrong' answers. Open-ended questions, however, lead children to think about their work more carefully. 'Tell me how you did that', or 'Try to explain to S------', are questions which help children think through their understanding and lead easily into the 'What would happen if . . .?' type of question.

AT 1: 3a

Children who have learnt to select their own apparatus and methods for tasks, and who are accustomed to discussing and questioning during their work, will be confident to look for alternative approaches when their initial attempt requires further consideration. They will notice and discuss difficulties and make suggestions to each other which will further develop their learning processes.

AT1:3b From the earliest stages of classroom mathematics correct mathematical language should be used, and systematic working and recording (when appropriate) are essential to ensure that clear and accurate information can be conveyed. There are words and phrases, such as 'and', or 'the difference', which are in common usage, and which have specific meanings in mathematics. Frequent use in mathematical situations will enable children to remember and use such terms with confidence.

AT1:3c Simple and straightforward recording helps children to maintain clarity in their work. The complexity can be increased as the children become more systematic and confident in the presentation of their results.

AT1:3d Predictions other than guesses can only be based on experience and thought. Children who have been taught to discuss, question and think about their work will naturally begin with an approximation of where their answer may fall. The question 'What do you expect?', or 'What did you expect?' will encourage them to think carefully about what they are doing and ensure that they are not on 'automatic pilot', unaware of how reasonable or not is the approach or answer they are offering.

Specific activities related to 'using and applying mathematics' are not appropriate. As previously mentioned, the first Attainment Target relates to the way in which children work rather than to what they learn. Consequently, all the activities suggested are designed to be conducted within a framework which encompasses the suggestions in this chapter, encouraging children to think through their work, to select their own materials, to use correct language, to work systematically, to discuss and question: that is to be active participants in their own learning.

$11+49=60$ Number

ACTIVITY 1

AT 2: 1a

Equipment
a wide variety of objects for counting
and addition

Provide unusual objects for children to use in counting
and addition, in a context which is appropriate for the
time of year or topic. This will maintain their interest
and help them to see mathematics as a way of finding
answers rather than just a school task. Encourage them
to use acorns, conkers, sweets, sultanas, satsumas and
so on, as well as the more traditionally recognised cubes
or counters.

ACTIVITY 2

AT 2: 2a

Equipment
10 linking cubes, e.g. multilink or unifix

Play the 'Magic number' game. Show the children that
you have a stick of 10 linking cubes, then hide them
behind your back or under a cloth on your knee. Break
the stick and keep the 'magic number' part hidden.
Show the children the broken-off section, count the
cubes with them and ask them to 'guess' the magic
number. Frequent sessions of this quickly build up
number bond recall.

With more able children, use higher numbers and
encourage quicker responses.

ACTIVITY 3

AT 2: 2a

Equipment
2 dice – the bigger the better, objects for
adding up

Throw the two dice. Add the numbers together, initially

with the help of objects, eventually as a quick mental exercise.

ACTIVITY 4

Equipment
a prepared set of 22 cards, with a number from 0 to 10 on one side of each card (two of each number)

AT 2: 2a

Children will enjoy this game as they become more confident at adding numbers up to 10. Shuffle the cards, and spread them out face down in random order. Play the game of 'Pairs', initially matching the numbers, but move quickly on to pairs that make a total of 10, such as 6 and 4, or 8 and 2. In turn, each child turns up two cards. If they make a pair, the child keeps them and has another turn. If they do not make a pair, the cards are returned to the same place on the table or floor. The game encourages memory and quick recall of number pairs. For more able children, prepare a set of cards which add up to 20 (or any other number).

AT 2: 3a

ACTIVITY 5

Equipment
the same set of cards as Activity 4

AT 2: 2a

This can be done in occasional five-minute slots, or with a small group in a more concentrated way. Shuffle the cards so that they are in random order. Hold up one card, asking a particular child to respond with the matching number to make 10 (or any number chosen by the teacher). Again, this is encouraging quick recall of number bonds, and can increase in difficulty as the children become more proficient at it. Maintaining the atmosphere of a game is very important, and children who find it difficult can be given apparatus or extra time.

AT 2: 3a

ACTIVITY 6

AT 2: 2a

Equipment
a set of number cards,
⊞ and ⊟ cards in another colour

Ask the children to invent their own sums using the cards, setting them out on the table for checking before they record them. They can do their own checking with a calculator.

ACTIVITY 7

AT 2: 2a, 3a

Equipment
a similar set of cards, including ⊟ cards as well

Again, the children can invent their own sums which can be checked before recording. Number cards can go up to 10 or 20, depending on the ability of the children.

ACTIVITY 8

Equipment
2 (or 4) cards prepared as shown, 2 dice (marked 1 to 6), a box of linking cubes or some counters

3	11	4	6
7	5	12	10
9	6	2	8

AT 2: 2a

A game for 2 or 4 children. In turn, the children throw the dice, add the numbers shown and place the appropriate size tower of cubes on the correct space. Alternatively, placing a counter on the space indicates that the total has been thrown. The winner is the first to cover all the spaces.

ACTIVITY 9

Equipment
a set of 9 cards containing numbers, words, and symbols:

| + | − | = | is | 5 | 3 | 2 |

| more than | less than |

AT 2: 2a

Ask the children to make true statements using the cards, such as:

| 5 | = | 3 | + | 2 |

| 5 | − | 3 | = | 2 |

| 2 | is | 3 | less than | 5 |

| 5 | is | 3 | more than | 2 |

Vary the numbers or symbols, or provide more than three numbers, according to the ability of the children.

ACTIVITY 10

Equipment
the class registers

AT 2: 3a

Each day, discuss the various combinations within the class, and do addition and subtraction sums around the figures they offer:

- children present + children absent

- children in the class − children absent

- children present − home dinners

Find any other natural subdivisions of the class which provide opportunities for addition or subtraction.

ACTIVITY 11

Equipment

a set of two-sided cards, with 0 to 10 on one side, and sums on the reverse (the sets shown are an example, but others can be made up as required)

Side 1	Side 2
0	5 + 2
1	10 − 5
2	7 − 6
3	9 − 7
4	3 − 3
5	3 + 5
6	7 + 2
7	5 − 2
8	6 + 4
9	3 + 1
10	2 + 4

AT 2 : 2a

Share out all the cards, with only the answers showing, and play 'Number trains'. Start with the answer 3. The child who has 3 reads out the sum on the back, and the child with the answer to that sum reads out the sum on the back of his or her card. Continue until it gets back to 3.

AT 2 : 3a, 3b

Once the children are good at this, time the group to see if they can get faster. The same activity can be used with larger numbers, with individual times tables, or with mixed tables to encourage quick recall of bonds. Each set of cards needs careful planning to ensure that each answer only occurs once, and that all the cards are used in turn.

15

ACTIVITY 12

Equipment
blank '100 squares'

1	2	3	4
11	12	13	14
21	22	23	24
31	32	33	34

AT 2: 2a

Ask the children to fill in the square with numbers to 100.

AT 2: 3a

AT 3: 3a

The activity can then be used for children to colour every second square, fifth square, or tenth square. Discuss the pattern made by each. Ask them to write the numbers in each pattern to draw their attention to the individual numbers. Discuss the 2, 5 or 10 times tables and the numbers which occur in each. Particularly encourage them to notice the units digit of each number in each pattern or table.

ACTIVITY 13

Equipment
a large number of sweets, cubes or other relevant small objects, and a number line to 100

AT 2: 2a

Ask the children to group the objects in 10s, then work out how many objects there are all together. Ask them to find that number on the number line and to decide which '10' the number is nearest to. Discuss how many more would be needed to reach the next '10'.

ACTIVITY 14

Equipment
cards with random numbers to 100

AT 2: 3d

As the children become familiar with different numbers in the previous activity, work without the objects, using cards prepared with numbers below 100 instead. Begin with numbers such as 39 and 81, which are close to a '10' as these are more obvious. Continue to 26, 54 and so on, as they become more confident.

Extend this to numbers above 100 when children can confidently handle numbers below 100. Begin by asking the children for a number close to 300, 700 and so on, then discuss which is the nearest '100' for 207, 398 and other numbers close to the hundred. Only move to numbers such as 273 or 428 when the children show that they are ready.

Offer worksheets in this area once the children show a firm grasp of the practical aspect of the activity.

ACTIVITY 15   *Equipment*
children themselves

Help the children to understand the 2 × table by looking at themselves:

AT 2: 3c

1 child   has 2 eyes
2 children have 4 eyes
3 children have 6 eyes
4 children have 8 eyes, etc.

Adapt any situation which seems appropriate, such as arms, legs, ears, pairs of socks, birds' legs or wings.

Draw the sets before recording with numbers and symbols.

1 child

2 eyes

2 children

4 eyes

3 children

6 eyes

17

For the $5 \times$ table, use sets of fingers on a hand, petals on a flower, points on a star, sides on a pentagon, chocolate biscuits in a pack, doors on a five-door car.

For the $10 \times$ table, use sets of fingers, toes, sweets in a packet.

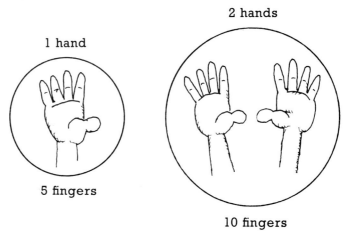

2 hands

1 hand

5 fingers

10 fingers

ACTIVITY 16

Equipment
apples, biscuits, cakes, sweets, paper

Take any opportunities in the classroom to share things in real situations:

AT 2: 2c

- $\frac{1}{2}$ or $\frac{1}{4}$ of an apple, small cake or biscuit, or pancakes on pancake day,

- share 6 sweets between 2 children and make it clear that they have half the number each,

- share 2 biscuits or jam tarts between 4 children,

- fold a piece of paper into halves in order to draw daytime and night-time pictures, or into quarters to draw pictures of the four seasons.

As children understand the concept of halves and quarters in real situations they will find it easier to transfer their knowledge to abstract number situations and come to know that half of 10 is 5.

ACTIVITY 17   *Equipment*
linking cubes, beads and laces

AT 2: 2c   Ask the children to make sticks or thread beads of a certain number (always use an even number), using only two colours, so that half are one colour and half are the other colour.

Record the task in pictures and/or numbers:

6 cubes

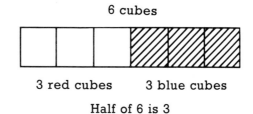

3 red cubes   3 blue cubes

Half of 6 is 3

or:

8 cubes

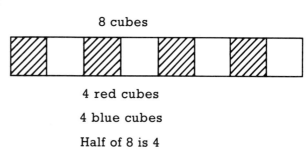

4 red cubes

4 blue cubes

Half of 8 is 4

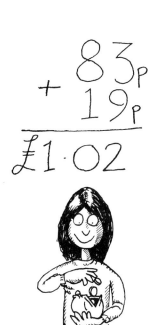

$$\begin{array}{r} 83_p \\ +\ 19_p \\ \hline £1\cdot 02 \end{array}$$

Money

Take any opportunities for children to handle real money. Counting real amounts of money for a specific purpose provides tremendous motivation and learning which cannot be equalled.

Ask children to check their own contribution for a school trip as well as perhaps counting the daily or final total. Similarly, ask them to check their money and change for books for a book club or during a book week.

Encourage contributions of small coins for charity collections, organise real sales of second-hand books or toys, sell squash or fruit at break, sell the results of class cooking. Experiencing real money and change in real situations will provide very effective incidental learning.

ACTIVITY 18

Equipment
prepared sets of cards or dominoes

Using commercially produced gummed paper coins, make sets of dominoes, or cards for 'pairs', at different levels.

AT 2: 2b

- Make a set of cards or dominoes which show single coins, to develop coin recognition.

- Make a second set with coins and names (1p, 5p) for matching the coin to the name.

- A further set could show groups of coins (such as 2p, 5p, 20p) and matching amounts (27p) so that children need to add up and match the coins to the correct amounts.

- Another set could show more than one coin on each section up to varying amounts within 10p, 20p, 50p or £1, depending on the ability of the children. To play this, children must add the amounts and match to a similar amount made up with different coins.

ACTIVITY 19

Equipment
an object (such as an apple or pencil) and a realistic price tag, token coins, small pots or circles of paper

AT 2: 2b

Place the object and price tag in the centre of the table, with the pots or papers around it. Ask the children to suggest different ways of paying for the object, putting the different combinations of coins in the pots or on the papers.

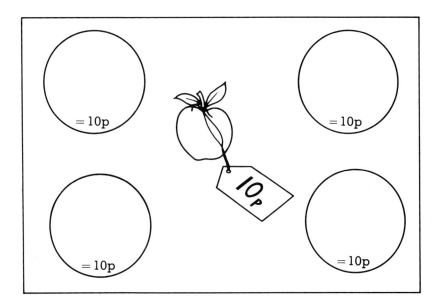

Vary the activity to provide practice with appropriate amounts of money for the children concerned.

Once the children are familiar with the activity, they can record their work on a worksheet laid out in a similar way.

ACTIVITY 20

Equipment

2 or 4 prepared cards as shown, token coins or real coins, a money dice

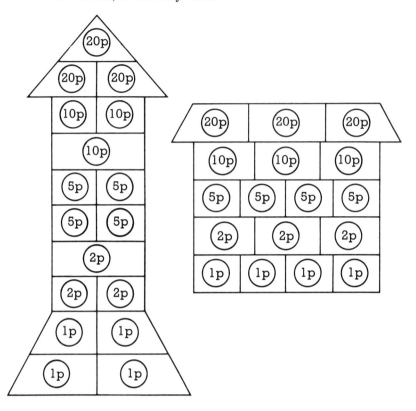

Any shape appropriate to the time of year or topic will encourage enthusiasm in the children.

AT 2: 2a, 3e Use commercially produced gummed coins to stick on to each shape a selection of coins which add up to the same amount. In turn the children throw the money dice, and place on their shape the amount of money shown. The rules can make this a straightforward matching game so that the turn is void if the particular coins are already covered. Alternatively, the game can be planned so that exchange of coins may be necessary to complete it.

The game can be varied by using higher value coin pictures on the shapes and two money dice, requiring the use of the skills of addition and exchange of money.

ACTIVITY 21

Equipment
a class shop

There are many possibilities in a class shop for handling real as well as token money. Stimulate interest by changing the shop regularly, such as a sweet shop, toy shop, bakery, greengrocer, cafe or restaurant, second-hand bookshop.

Price the items in the shop at levels which enable extensions of the free-play opportunities into structured money and shopping activities. Give children a specific amount of money and specify what they should buy.

Use this type of activity to check either the total amount or the change (or both). Ask the children to buy:

AT 2: 2b

a chew	3p
a toffee	2p
TOTAL	___

or

a sandwich	65p
a cake	30p
a drink	10p
TOTAL	___

or

AT 2: 3e

3 oranges at 15p each	45p
2 apples at 12p each	24p
4 bananas at 10p each	40p
TOTAL	___

Use coins to help understanding. Introduce the concept of change from 10p at first, moving on to 20p, 50p and £1 as children show that they are ready.

Provide workcards or worksheets alongside a shop or cafe situation, designed so that children can vary what they buy within a predetermined structure:

AT 2: 2b

I started with	20p

I bought	Cost
a pencil	7p
a rubber	5p
TOTAL	12p

CHANGE 8p

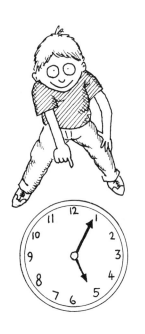

Length, Weight and Time

There are endless opportunities in life outside school to help children to learn and understand about metres, miles, kilograms, pints and so on. It is important that some of these situations be introduced into the classroom.

AT 1:1c

A timetable marked with particular times in the day or week of gym, hall, TV or video times encourages children to notice the time and remember what happens on a particular day. From time to time make a point of discussing what happened the day before, or what will happen that afternoon, tomorrow or next week.

A calendar marked with birthdays, holidays, outings, visitors and any other significant events will help children to understand the passing of months and years, and to remember the date of their own birthday.

AT 2:2d

Discuss with the class distances to each others' houses, to the nearest shops, or the nearest town in terms of miles. Ask them to look at the mileometer on a car and encourage them to talk to their parents about distances when they visit friends, relations or go on holiday.

If the class is going out of school by coach, discuss the distance and how long the journey will take. Include leaving and arrival times and, if appropriate, reasons for a coach journey taking longer than a car journey to the same place.

AT 2: 2d

In a topic about people at work, involve the milkman who delivers pints of milk, the garage which sells litres of petrol and the supermarket which sells sugar in 1 kg packets and butter in 250 g ($\frac{1}{4}$ kg) packets. Look at jars of jam, tins of fruit, packets of cereal and ask the children to find the weights marked on them.

AT 2: 2d, 3e

A regular cooking session (involving areas of the Science and the Design and Technology documents) can help children to understand the use of grams, temperature and minutes. Make blancmanges and jellies using a pint of milk or water, or pancakes on pancake day.

ACTIVITY 22

Equipment
spring bulbs growing in a pot, rulers

AT 2: 2d

Plant indoor spring bulbs and keep them in the dark until they have started to grow. Once they are in the classroom, measure the growth of daffodil or hyacinth leaves each day. Make a chart or graph of the measurements.

At other times of the year, plant bean seeds in a jar with blotting paper, or cress seeds in cotton wool, and record the growth of the stems.

ACTIVITY 23

Equipment
two Babygros of different sizes, tape measures or rulers

AT 2: 2d

Ask the children to compare the two sizes of Babygro, measuring arm length, leg length, body length and width. They could record their results as a chart and discuss where the greatest differences come and which bits of a baby are expected to grow fastest.

ACTIVITY 24

Equipment
Jack and the Beanstalk,
Alice in Wonderland,
Mrs Pepperpot

AT 2: 2d, 3e

In the context of these stories, or work about 'change', use the concept of shrinking (*Alice in Wonderland, Mrs Pepperpot*) or growing (*Jack and the Beanstalk, Alice in Wonderland*). Ask the children how tall they would be if they shrank or grew by 1 m, 50 cm etc.

Make a model beanstalk which grows by a metre a day, and perhaps vary the rate of growth of the branches so that they grow more slowly. Ask them to make leaves which measure different lengths for different parts of the beanstalk, or a door for Alice to go through if she measured only 20 cm high. Compare the height of the table with the 'Drink me' bottle on it with Alice's height once she had shrunk.

ACTIVITY 25

Equipment
paint and paper, bowl of water, soap and towel

AT 2: 3e

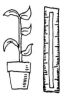

In the context of work about themselves, ask each child to do a hand print and a foot print and measure the length of each. Display these along with other information about themselves – their height, weight, age, birthday, baby photograph, and so on.

ACTIVITY 26

Equipment
three-dimensional objects, such as apples, oranges, stones, tomatoes (perhaps home-grown)

How many ways can these objects be measured?

AT 2: 2d, 3e

Children can measure the weight in non-standard or standard units, they can measure the circumference with a tape measure or a piece of wool which must then be measured, and they can measure the width with calipers.

Each measurement could be preceded with an estimate, or the results of several objects could be recorded in a chart. Ask the children to discover whether or not the heaviest object is the largest in any other way.

ACTIVITY 27

Equipment
several polythene bags (all the same size), a collection of objects or substances of varying weights such as pegs, nails, washers, cotton wool, beads, cubes, feathers, water, sawdust, sugar or dried peas

AT 2: 2d, 3e

Ask the children to weigh out 100 g of each object or substance and put the quantity weighed into a polythene bag and close it securely. Display the bags on a washing line so that they can see how much space is taken up by 100 g of cotton wool, or nails, or washers, and so on.

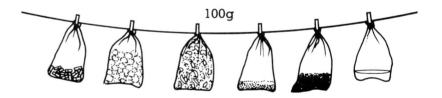
100g

Vary the task by asking them to weigh out 10 g or 50 g, always taking the opportunity to point out the differences in volume for the same weight.

ACTIVITY 28

Equipment
a selection of parcels packed in brown paper addressed for the post

Perhaps in December, when families are thinking of

AT 2: 2d,3e

posting Christmas parcels, ask the children to compare the weights of the parcels without the scales at first, then using scales. Ask them to put them in order of weight or to weigh them accurately in grams.

Discuss with them suggestions for items which would be light or heavy to post, and consequently more or less appropriate to send as Christmas presents.

ACTIVITY 29

Equipment
a classroom clock with a seconds hand, or
a minute timer, or a stop clock

AT 2: 2d

Ask the children to choose one child to watch the clock while the rest of them close their eyes and estimate the passing of a minute. They can raise their hand or open their eyes when they judge a minute has gone. They will get better at this with practice.

Estimation

Estimating is a much underrated aspect of mathematics. It helps us to have a 'feel' for the approximate answer to expect when dealing with large numbers or complex situations, and involves much more thought than a mere guess at the answer. Estimation is a skill which develops with experience. An essential part of estimation in the classroom is the checking afterwards, so that children can improve and refine subsequent estimates in the light of experience.

ACTIVITY 30

Equipment
counters, cubes, marbles, sweets, or similar small objects, small dishes or pots

AT 2:1a

Put a handful of small objects on a dish, and ask the children to estimate how many there are. When all the children have made a suggestion, ask them if they are happy with what they have said, or if anyone would like to adjust their estimate. Once they are all happy, ask someone to count how many there are and discuss who was nearest. Repeat the same activity several times with different numbers, giving the children the experience needed to improve their skills.

Vary the objects used, so that they begin to generalise their estimation skills, and gradually increase the number up to about 20.

ACTIVITY 31

Equipment
cubes, acorns, wheels, washers or other small objects, a variety of small containers such as egg cups or yogurt pots

Work initially with only one group of small objects, extending to other objects when the children are estimating confidently and are ready to generalise.

AT 2: 1a Start by picking up just a few objects in a closed fist and ask the children to guess how many there are. Ask them again with the hand open so that they can see the objects, but not count. Compare the ease of estimating when they can or cannot see the objects. Make the activity into an informal game, encouraging discussion when the estimates vary, and always asking them to count the objects to check their estimates.

AT 2: 3d Show the children a variety of small containers and ask them to estimate how many of the same objects would fit in each one. Check the accuracy of their estimates by counting.

AT 5: 2a, 3b As an alternative approach to this activity, use just one, slightly larger container. Ask a group of children to devise a data collection sheet on which to record each child's estimate of how many objects would fill the container. Use that data to construct a bar chart to show the variations in estimates (some children may want to revise their estimates at this stage). This may offer the opportunity to discuss the shape of the distribution of estimates and the range shown. Checking the accuracy of the estimation and comparing that with the chart will identify the levels of skill within the class.

ACTIVITY 32 *Equipment*
a tube of Smarties, a saucer or small dish

AT 2: 3d Put all of the Smarties from the tube into a dish or saucer so that the children can see them well. Ask them to estimate how many blue Smarties there are, how many red ones and so on. Help them to compare their suggestions, estimate which colour is most or least. After discussion, ask them to count and make a bar chart or a block graph.

AT 5: 2a,3b As an addition to this activity, ask the children to record the estimates for one of the colours and use the information to make a graph. The discussion provoked by seeing a pattern of estimates around the actual figure will help to lead children to more refined estimating.

ACTIVITY 33

Equipment
a transparent container, water, marbles

AT 2: 3d

Fill the transparent container almost to the top with water and stand it in a dish or saucer. Ask the children to write down how many marbles they think will fit into the container with the water before the water spills. Again, discussion of their estimates, a chance to revise their estimates in the light of other suggestions, or a graph of the estimates, will serve to further develop their skills. Add marbles to the container one at a time until the water spills, and discuss the variations between their estimates and the actual number. As their estimation skills improve, use different sized objects which will sink and displace the water (such as nails, stones, rubbers or paper clips).

Develop this activity by using a standard volume of water in a standard container and different objects. Ask the children to construct a bar chart of the results and suggest reasons for the differences.

$$\begin{array}{r} 37 \\ +28 \\ \hline 65 \end{array}$$

Place Value

Place value is one of the hardest concepts in mathematics, yet children are rarely given sufficient practical experience before being asked to work with numbers in the abstract. If a true understanding is achieved, children have few difficulties with the relative values of digits within a number, and will find that work with tens and units and higher numbers suddenly makes sense!

ACTIVITY 34

AT 2: 3a, 4a, 4b

Equipment
several packets of Fruitella sweets

Fruitellas come in ones
or in packets of 10.

Anyone wanting to buy 36 Fruitellas must buy
3 packets and 6 more.

Anyone wanting to buy 25 Fruitellas must buy
2 packets and 5 more.

This can be extended to

single sweets	1
packets of 10	10
bags of 10 packets	100
boxes of 10 bags	1000
crates of 10 boxes	10 000

Initially, discuss how many packets and single sweets will make up a number, and how many sweets there are in a given number of packets of sweets.

Consider the factory working out how many packets they will get from a number of sweets and how many will be left as single sweets, or how many sweets they have put into a batch of packets and singles.

Using this analogy, children readily understand that once there are 10 sweets a packet can be made, and that once there are 10 packets a bag can be made. It takes little development to move on to the fact that

```
         2 packets and 6 singles (26 sweets)
added to 1 packet  and 7 singles (17 sweets)
         gives 4 packets and 3 singles (43 sweets)
as there are enough singles to create an extra
packet, leaving 3 singles
```

This concept also helps with the decomposition approach to subtraction.

AT 2: 3a,4a,4b

Rebecca has 4 packets and 5 singles (45 sweets)

She wants to give enough to her teacher for one each for the 28 children in her class. She can only do this by opening a new packet.

```
          4 packets and 5 singles
minus     2 packets and 8 singles
leaves    1 packet  and 7 singles
```

Similarly, place value can be seen in terms of bananas, which come in

singles	1
bunches of 10	10
boxes of 10 bunches	100
crates of 10 boxes	1000
lorry loads of 10 crates	10 000

or even money, which comes in

pennies	1p
10p coins	10p
£1 coins	100p
£10 notes	1000p

ACTIVITY 35

Equipment

raindrops (from blue paper), clouds (from grey paper), a 1 to 6 dice

In the context of the weather, play the 'Rain game'.

AT 2: 3a,4a,4b

In turn, children throw the dice and collect raindrops according to the number thrown. A collection of 10 raindrops is exchanged for a cloud, and a collection of 10 clouds makes a storm which is the end of the game.

This activity can have an extra level if puddles are included:

```
10 raindrops = 1 puddle
10 puddles   = 1 cloud
10 clouds    = 1 storm
```

It could be used in snowy weather:

```
10 snowflakes = 1 snowball
10 snowballs  = 1 snowman
10 snowmen    = 1 snowdrift
```

or in the context of flowers:

```
10 petals   = 1 flower
10 flowers  = 1 border
10 borders  = 1 garden
```

or children:

```
10 children = 1 team
10 teams    = 1 competition
```

The possibilities are endless, and the children enjoy each different game as a new activity.

The activity can be varied by imposing a time limit and working out how many raindrops, snowflakes or petals they have won in the time by using the place value of the various stages of the game.

ACTIVITY 36

Equipment

2 or 4 money cards as shown, money dice with amounts less than 10p, real or token coins

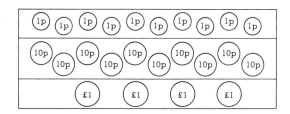

AT 2: 3a, 3e, 4b

In turn, the children throw the dice, and collect the amount shown, placing penny coins on the pennies on the card. When all the penny spaces are filled they exchange 10 pennies for a 10p coin. When all the 10p spaces are filled, ten 10p coins are changed for a £1 coin. The game can finish when all the £1 spaces are filled, when all the spaces are filled, or when a stated time has elapsed, at which point the winner is the player with the most money.

ACTIVITY 37

Equipment
paper and pencil, calculator

AT 2: 3a

Ask the children to make up as many sums as possible to which the answer is 100. Offer extra incentives for sums which use multiplication or division rather than just addition and subtraction.

ACTIVITY 38

Equipment
paper and pencil, the current 'year' number, calculator

Discuss how many

AT 2: 3a, 4b

    thousands
    hundreds
    tens
    units

there are in the current year.

As in Activity 37, ask the children to make up as many sums as they can to which the answer is the year number, offering similar incentives.

ACTIVITY 39

Equipment
a number line, a ten strip

AT 2: 3a

Give the children a list of starting points on the number line, and a ten strip. By placing the ten strip on the line on their starting number, they can add 10, and read off the answer from the number line. Children 'counting on' from 27 will naturally start at 28 and reach 37; the ten strip does the same.

Ask the children to record their starting point and their answer, encouraging them to see the pattern which results.

22	23	24	25	26	27	28	29	30	31	32	33	34	35	36	37	38	39

1	2	3	4	5	6	7	8	9	10

ACTIVITY 40

Equipment
paper and pencils, calculator

Take the children into the school car park to write down all the registration numbers of the cars.

AT 2: 3a

Back in the classroom, extract just the two or three numbers from each registration number. Discuss which is the smallest number, which is the largest, and which digit in the numbers gives that information.

Encourage the children to notice numbers with the same 10s digit or the same 100s digit. Look for the number closest to 300, 400, and so on.

Put each number on a separate piece of paper and ask the children to put them in ascending or descending order.

Cut one of the numbers up into separate digits and rearrange the digits to make the smallest or largest number possible using all three digits. Discuss which digit is the most important in this situation.

Using the same number, make all the possible three-digit numbers, and place them in ascending or descending order. Again, discuss the relative importance of the different digits.

AT 2: 4a Add the digits of each number. Which is the highest or lowest? Is this the same number as the highest or lowest number?

AT 2: 3b Which numbers can be divided by 2, 5, 10?

AT 2: 3a, 4a Use the numbers from the cars for addition and subtraction (using a calculator) to discover the differences between the numbers. For children moving towards level 4, ask them to do this addition and subtraction without a calculator.

Collect the registration numbers of family cars for the class to do the same activities on a different set of numbers.

ACTIVITY 41   *Equipment*
                       structured apparatus, such as Dienes

AT 3: 3a This activity helps children to understand that the answer will be the same, whichever way the addition is done, provided their work is accurate.

Consider $32 + 45$.

What happens if they add the units first, then the tens?

$$2 + 5 = 7$$
$$30 + 40 = 70$$
$$\overline{}$$
$$77$$
$$\overline{}$$

What happens if they add the tens, then the units?

$$30 + 40 = 70$$
$$2 + 5 = 7$$
$$\overline{}$$
$$77$$
$$\overline{}$$

Or $26 + 18$

$6 + 8 = 14$	$20 + 10 = 30$
$20 + 10 = 30$	$6 + 8 = 14$
$\overline{}$	$\overline{}$
44	44
$\overline{}$	$\overline{}$

What happens if they 'add on' from the first number?

$$26 + 18$$
$$26 + 8 = 34, \ 34 + 10 = 44$$

AT 3:3a

AT 2:4a

Some children find this obvious and very easy. It requires an understanding of, and a facility with, numbers. As children practise breaking numbers down into the different component parts of tens and units, they will find that these approaches can offer a quick way of finding the answers.

-4 -3 -2 -1 0 1

Negative Numbers

Negative numbers are accepted as normal in temperatures, and can also be accepted as normal in the classroom if the number line starts below zero. We want children to understand that numbers are a continuum that begins somewhere in the past and continues ever onwards. We deal mostly with those numbers close to and above zero, but also sometimes with those below zero.

ACTIVITY 42

Equipment
number line

Introduce at an early stage the concept that numbers do not start or finish, and that 0 is not the beginning but a position in the number line.

⁻8	⁻7	⁻6	⁻5	⁻4	⁻3	⁻2	⁻1	0	1	2	3	4	5	6	7	8

AT 2: 3e

Ask the children to

```
start at 3, jump back 4
start at 2, jump back 5
start at 4, jump back 8
start at 2, jump back 9
```

Recording this activity becomes rather confusing as children often forget to include the minus sign. The practical activity is sufficient to enable them to understand the concept of negative numbers.

ACTIVITY 43

Equipment
an outdoor thermometer

AT 2: 3e In the context of the weather, or winter, in the late Autumn or early Spring term, take daily outdoor temperature readings and make a line graph with the results.

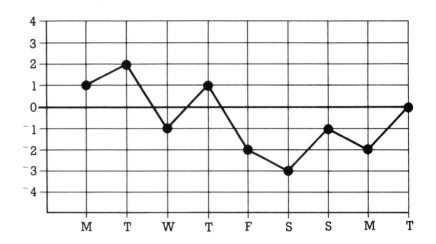

 Discuss with the children the temperature differences between (in this example) Tuesday and Wednesday, Wednesday and Thursday, Friday and Saturday. Discuss the fact that the difference between -2 and -3 is 1: there is a 1 degree difference. More able children may notice that $2-(-1)$ is the same as $2+1$. Encourage them to notice that the difference between 3 and -2 is 5 degrees.

ACTIVITY 44

Equipment
none

AT 2: 3e In the context of offices or shops, discuss the idea of above and below ground floors. Using the ground floor as 0, how far must a lift travel from floor 2 above ground level to floor -1 below ground?

ACTIVITY 45

Equipment
calculators

AT 2: 3e Check that the school calculators show negative numbers on the display in a way that the children can understand.

As part of a discussion about calculators, ask the children what they think the calculator will display if they ask it to calculate a sum such as $3-5$. They may be able to think of other sums which will give the same $-$ sign. Try larger numbers ($27-48$). Explain the results in the context of the number line going backwards.

ACTIVITY 46

Equipment
a game board as shown, a coin, a score sheet, a counter or other playing piece

AT 2: 3e This game can be played alone or with a partner. Start the scoring at 2. Put the counter on 'Start', and toss the coin. Move right one square if it lands 'Heads', and down one square if it lands 'Tails'.

If the counter finally lands on 'Finish', score 2 points. If the counter goes off the board, score -1 point, which may take the score into negative numbers. Return to 'Start' for another turn. The aim of the game is to score 10 points.

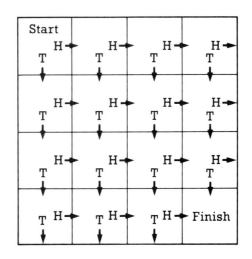

H = Heads

T = Tails

6 2 6 ✿ 6 2

Algebra

In the past pattern-making has been associated with early mathematics rather than with algebra. All numbers make patterns, and it is the use of pattern in number which makes mathematics so powerful. It is algebra which takes the pattern in number and uses that pattern to explain so many things which would otherwise continue to be a mystery.

ACTIVITY 47

Equipment
coloured beads, laces

AT 3:1a

At the simplest level, ask children to make repeating patterns of coloured beads, compare the patterns, and extend a pattern of

    red, blue, red, blue, red . . .

or

    red, red, blue, blue, red, red, blue, blue . . .

or further,

    red, red, blue, red, red, blue . . .

or

    red, blue, blue, green, red, blue, blue, green . . .

Encourage more complex patterns, devising patterns for children to copy and continue, and asking them to devise patterns for others to copy and continue.

Extend pattern-making into other areas, according to the topic of study at the time. Thread a pattern of conkers and leaves in the Autumn, make patterns of colours or shapes to link with other areas of mathematics. Use alternating or more complex patterns to make borders round the edge of greetings cards, invitations, or other writing, or use handwriting to make patterns (b d f f b d f f).

ACTIVITY 48

Equipment
a selection of objects which offer two or three variations, such as buttons, coins or fruit

AT 3: 1a

Devise patterns which are of particular interest to the children, using objects such as buttons, coins or fruit. Use items or drawings which link to other work in the classroom, such as shells and pebbles, snowmen and scarves, trees and stars, sun and moon, hats and handbags. Ask the children to copy and continue the patterns, or devise patterns themselves for others to copy and continue.

ACTIVITY 49

Equipment
sewing equipment, paint and potatoes for printing

AT 3: 1a

Use stitching or potato printing as ways of encouraging children to devise and practise pattern making. Potato printing can be used to make wrapping paper, or a border round a large classroom picture; stitching can be used to create a bookmark in book week, or mounted on to a card for Mothers' Day.

ACTIVITY 50

Equipment
objects as above, pencil, paper, colours

AT 3: 2b

Use coloured cubes or squares, leaving spaces in the pattern for the child to complete. Later, prepare patterns as already suggested, using numbers, colours, shapes or objects. Substitute a cloud shape or box in the space to be filled in. Ask the child to look carefully at the pattern, decide what is missing and fill in the cloud or box. This has two purposes: firstly to help them recognise that the cloud or box has a hidden meaning which they can discover, and secondly to encourage them to spot how the repeating pattern works.

3   5   3   5 ⛅ 5   3   5   3 ⛅ 3   5

ACTIVITY 51

Equipment
a group of children

AT 3: 2a

This activity can be used in the spare few minutes which occur just before playtime or lunch time. Ask perhaps 6 children to stand together in front of the class, and ask the class how many children there are. Split one of the 6 slightly away from the other 5 and discuss the sum

$$5 + 1 = 6$$

Move a second child to join the first, and discuss the sum

$$4 + 2 = 6$$

Move a third child to join the other two, and discuss

$$3 + 3 = 6$$

Continue until all 6 children are together again, creating the sum

$$6 + 0 = 6$$

Go through the activity again, quickly, encouraging the children to notice the patterns created within 6.

This can, of course, be done with any number, and provides a practical way to demonstrate pattern in addition. The same technique can be used to explore patterns in subtraction, and different groupings of numbers within a number.

ACTIVITY 52

Equipment
none

Set out work in as many different forms as possible, encouraging children to think carefully about what is needed to fill the gaps.

$$3 + \square = 7, \quad \square + 4 = 7, \quad 3 + 4 = \square$$

$$
\begin{array}{ccc}
3 & 3 & \square \\
+\,4 & +\,\square & +\,4 \\
\hline
=\,\square & =\,7 & =\,7
\end{array}
$$

AT 3: 2b Develop the ability to complete the sum as well as find the answer so that children understand that the box or cloud symbol represents an unknown number. Move them away from the conditioned response that the 'answer goes in the box' towards the need to find out what is missing to make the sum correct.

ACTIVITY 53

Equipment
none

AT 3: 2a Prepare simple addition and subtraction sums with the + or − sign missing. Ask the children to be detectives, and work out which sign is needed to make the sum correct. Encourage them to work out the sum they decide on, developing a system of self-checking.

ACTIVITY 54

Equipment
linking cubes, a large box

AT 3: 3b Make a function machine to 'add 2'.

Cut the flaps off the box, and make a hole in each end. Place the open side of the box facing one child, and a child at each end of the box, next to each hole. The child at one end needs a collection of linking cubes, and the child in the middle needs pairs of similar cubes.

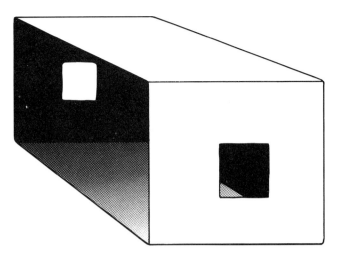

Ask the first child to pass 3 cubes 'through' the
machine. The child in the middle must always add
2 cubes, and pass the correct number (5) out through the
opposite side.

Do the same with 1 cube, then 6 cubes, building up
a pattern for the children to see the effect of the
'machine'.

Change the function of the machine to 'add 6', or
'subtract 3', or 'multiply by 2'.

Discuss what would happen if the machine went wrong
and started to pass the numbers backwards. It would
perform the opposite calculation. Pass 4 cubes into an
'add 2 machine' which passes 6 cubes out. Then pass
the 6 cubes back in through the wrong end, take the
2 cubes away again, passing the 4 cubes back out to the
beginning.

AT 3: 4a This works particularly well to demonstrate the concept
of doubling and halving. Pass 2 cubes into a 'doubling
machine' which passes 4 cubes out. Working backwards,
the 4 cubes are reduced back to 2.

ACTIVITY 55

Equipment
none

AT 3: 3b, 4a

In PE, practise 'inverse operations' by moving in one direction, then moving in the reverse direction. With the children in individual spaces facing the front, ask them to take 2 steps forward, then 2 steps backwards to where they started. Ask them to move 3 paces to the right then 3 paces to the left, or to sit down then stand up. Doing these actions facing in the same direction rather than changing direction for the 'inverse operation' helps them to understand the concept of 'undoing' something they have just 'done'. Explain it in the context of a car or a sewing machine going forward then reversing. In the same way we can reverse things in mathematics: we can add a number then we can take it away again, we can multiply by 5 then we can divide by 5, to get back to the original number.

Shape and Space

When the children have had a wide experience of working with 2D and 3D shapes with bricks, box modelling and other activities, they will begin to observe differences in the shapes. A wide variety of shapes freely available will encourage incidental learning to a level at which children are ready to learn the names of each of the different shapes they can identify. In the course of such activities, encourage them to discuss the shapes they are using, and the relative advantages and disadvantages of different shapes for different purposes.

ACTIVITY 56

Equipment
a variety of 2D or 3D shapes

Ask a small group of children to describe each shape in turn, considering size, corners (vertices), number of sides, length of sides, shape of faces and number of faces.

For 2D shapes, ask the children to try to fit several identical shapes together to cover the working surface. Discuss which shapes will tessellate (fit together without leaving any spaces).

For 3D shapes, ask them to discover which shapes they can pile up and which they can roll. They could also sort them into groups, looking at flat surfaces, curved surfaces, faces of the same shape, and record their

findings in straight sets,

AT 4: 3a

as a Venn diagram,

AT 5: 2a

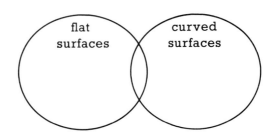

or in a more conventional table of facts.

Shape	Number of sides	Number of corners
△		
⬡		
⬠		

ACTIVITY 57

Equipment
a piece of paper (any shape), 2D and 3D shapes

AT 4: 2a

Show the children how to make a straight fold in their piece of paper, and a second fold which divides the first fold in half, giving a paper right-angle.

Show them how to use the paper right-angle to examine the 2D and 3D shapes and discover right-angles. Discuss those angles which are bigger or smaller than a right-angle. Ask them to take their paper right-angle around the classroom and find other right-angles in floor tiles, wall corners, tables and cupboards, as well as the mathematics area.

ACTIVITY 58

Equipment
none

AT 4:2a

In a PE lesson, where there is plenty of space, divide the children into groups of three and ask them to form themselves into a triangle, either standing up or lying down. Then change to groups of four and form a square, and the same or different groups to form a rectangle.

Discuss the properties of the shape, and any difficulties they found. Do the same in groups of five for a pentagon, and groups of six for a hexagon.

To encourage further thought with respect to these shapes, ask three children to form a square or hexagon, or four children to form a triangle or pentagon. They will need to use one or two arms in different directions, or lie down with legs bent to form a corner. The shapes will not be very regular, but the activity will help the children to think about the differences between the shapes.

ACTIVITY 59

Equipment
none

AT 4:2a

Consider the school playground. Ask to have 2D shapes painted on the playground or on a wall, or take the children outside with chalk to draw very large pentagons, hexagons, squares and so on. Place a child standing at each corner of a shape: discuss how many are needed. Ask children to line the sides of a particular shape so that they make a human circle, pentagon and so on.

If the shapes are large enough, play games asking the children to run to the shape with six sides, or the shape with four corners. This sort of activity will help them to remember the properties of each shape.

AT 2: 3b,4a Use the shapes to help with tables and multiplication practice:

one child on each side of a pentagon $= 1 \times 5$
two children on each side of a pentagon $= 2 \times 5$
three children on each side of a pentagon $= 3 \times 5$

Use a triangle for the three times table, a square for the four times and so on.

ACTIVITY 60

Equipment

AT 4: 2b

In the classroom, or in PE, ask the children to face in one specific direction and describe what they can see straight ahead. Ask them to turn all the way round, a complete turn, back to the way they were facing originally. Ask them to turn a half turn, so they face the opposite direction and describe what they can see, then quarter turns (right-angles).

In the hall or playground, start with all the children in spaces, facing one direction. Ask them to take 3 steps forward, turn through a right-angle, 2 steps forward, turn through 2 right-angles, 4 steps forward. Invent different patterns of movement so that they become accustomed to the mathematical terms and understand what they mean.

Ask the children to take turns giving directions to the class, encouraging them to use the same mathematical language themselves.

ACTIVITY 61

Equipment

AT 4: 2b

Again, in the hall or playground, set the class out as a grid.

```
*    *    *    *    *

*    *    *    *    *

*    *    *    *    *

*    *    *    *    *

*    *    *    *    *
```

Place a spare child next to another child at any point in the grid and give directions for moving around the grid:

    2 children forward
    turn left through 3 right-angles
    5 children forward
    turn right through 2 right-angles
    3 children forward

When they reach the end of the specified route, they change places with the child at that point in the grid, who becomes the next dragon, hunter, mouse or other character.

Add interest to the activity by asking another child to turn their back on the grid and give directions so that the end of the route will be less planned!

Discuss the clarity of the directions, and establish a policy about whether or not left and right must always refer to the front of the grid to avoid confusion.

Extend the activities by giving more than one instruction at a time, or by setting a destination which must be reached.

ACTIVITY 62

Equipment
rectangles of paper, or cuboid bricks, Lego figures or cars, dice

AT 4 : 2b

Ask the children to make a road or path with the paper or bricks. Specify how far it should go, and whether it should be straight or have a certain number of right-angle turns. Number the papers or bricks, and use the throw of a dice to determine the movement of a car or Lego figure along the path and round the corners. Extend the game by adding penalties or bonuses, and perhaps an alternative longer route, on which each throw of the dice is multiplied by 2 to allow faster progress.

Translate this into a diagram to provide cross-curricular links with Geography.

ACTIVITY 63

Equipment
objects with interesting shapes, or letter or number templates, or shapes made with cubes, 2 rectangles of paper bigger than the shapes or templates

AT 4 : 2b

Ask a child to place one shape or template on one of the paper rectangles in any position, and carefully notice the exact position. Ask them to move the shape to the exact same position, but on the other rectangle. This is straight movement (translation). Make patterns with translation movement from coloured paper cut in the shape of the template and stuck on to squares or rectangles of paper of another colour.

Use the same equipment for a similar activity involving turning movement (rotation). It is most effective if the shape or template is not a simple polygon. This time, ask the children to draw round the shape, then turn it round a little and draw round it again. More able children could turn it and draw round it several times to make a pattern, perhaps colouring each different 'turn' to make their work clearer. As before, patterns can be made by cutting the shape out of coloured paper several times and sticking them on to another coloured sheet in the 'turning' pattern.

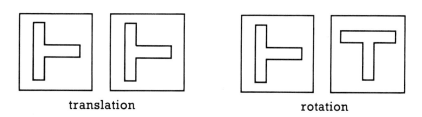

translation   rotation

AT 4: 3b A similar activity, drawing round the shape but turning it **over** before drawing it again, involves reflection. Again, slightly complex shapes are more effective than simple polygons.

ACTIVITY 64   *Equipment*
a selection of linking cubes, mirrors

AT 4: 3b Ask the children to make a stick of multicoloured cubes. When they place the mirror at one end of the stick, ask them to make up the reflection they can see. They can record their original stick and the reflection stick on squared paper.

Extend this activity by asking them to make more complex multicoloured shapes and the reflections, again perhaps recording their work on squared paper.

The children could set reflections for each other to construct and record, sustaining and developing the activity independently of the teacher.

ACTIVITY 65

Equipment
as in Activity 64

AT 4 : 3b	Children who are able to construct reflections as before can use the same linking cubes to make shapes which they believe are symmetrical in two or three dimensions. After discussing the lines of symmetry, they can check their work with a mirror.

ACTIVITY 66

Equipment
natural objects (e.g. leaves), wrapping paper, wallpaper

AT 4 : 2b	Encourage the children to find types of movement in the world around them. They will find translation and perhaps rotation in wallpaper and wrapping paper, and reflective symmetry in natural objects such as the inside halves of an apple or a tomato, or some of the more regular leaves.

ACTIVITY 67

Equipment
squared paper, crayons, or small squares of gummed coloured paper, mirror

AT 4 : 3b	Ask the children to draw a line across the middle of the paper, then create a coloured pattern to one side of the line. Tell them to place the mirror on the line to make the reflection and create the other half of the pattern so that it has reflective symmetry.

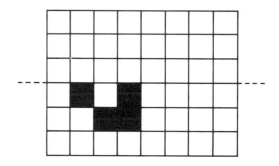

ACTIVITY 68

AT 4: 3b

Equipment
large sheets of paper, paints

Fold the paper in half and open it out. Ask the children to paint a pattern on one half of the paper. Fold the paper in half again while the paint it still wet and gently smooth over the top half. Open the paper out and the picture will have reflective symmetry.

ACTIVITY 69

Equipment
a game board as shown, compass point cards, dice marked 1, 1, 2, 2, 3, 3, counters, a simple compass or drawn compass directions

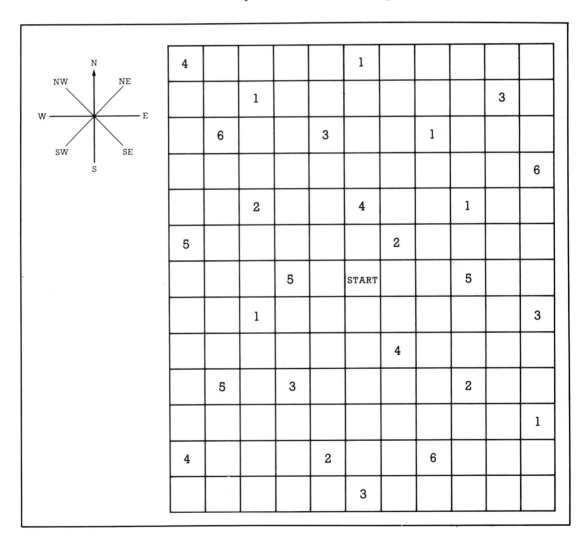

AT 4: 3c

The board is a large grid, with some squares which indicate a points score or number of items to collect. The START square should be the centre square of the grid. Provide a selection of compass point cards, randomly shuffled and in a pile upside down, and a dice marked 1, 1, 2, 2, 3, 3. Each player needs a counter or similar marker.

In turn, players take a compass point card and throw the dice. They move the correct number of spaces in the correct direction, scoring points or collecting items if they land on a numbered square. The game finishes if one player has to move off the board. The highest score wins.

Extend the activity by asking the children to keep a record of their moves, and draw their path later on a blank grid.

Handling Data

Opportunities to use data handling techniques arise continuously in the classroom. As the children become familiar with collecting and representing data, they will see more opportunities for using and refining those skills.

ACTIVITY 70

Equipment
none

AT 5:1

Ask the children if they know of someone who is going to have a baby, and discuss the possibilities of it being a boy or girl.

Help them, through discussion, to understand that every time a new baby is born, it will be either a boy or a girl.

Ask about older brothers or sisters, and emphasise the fact that the outcome last time has no effect on the outcome of the next occasion.

ACTIVITY 71

Equipment
a coin

AT 5:1

Work with just a small group of children, asking them in turn to toss the coin in the air. Each time discuss the way the coin lands, heads or tails uppermost. This activity is better done sitting round on the carpet to contain the coin, rather than at a table.

As above, emphasise the fact that each occasion can result in either heads or tails, and that the result of the last toss has no effect on the result of the next toss.

ACTIVITY 72   *Equipment*
a collection of objects, such as stamps, buttons, greetings cards, or shapes, a Carroll diagram

AT 5: 2a   Discuss with the children the various characteristics of the objects, emphasising the similarities and differences between the stamps, cards, etc. Together, select one characteristic, and sort the items into two groups: those with and those without that particular characteristic.

Then decide on another characteristic present in both of the first groups, and sort the two groups into four groups using the Carroll diagram.

Greetings cards	Animal	No animal
Pop-up		
Not pop-up		

As the children become familiar with this activity, they will be able to look at a prepared Carroll diagram, and place objects in the appropriate section without the initial two-group sort.

ACTIVITY 73   *Equipment*
objects as above, or use the children themselves, Venn diagram

AT 5: 2a   The Venn diagram is used for sorting items by characteristics which overlap, where one of the items belongs in two of the groupings.

Decide on two characteristics for the two sets, and label the sets. Consider each item in the whole group, and place it in the appropriate set. Items which do not belong in either set remain outside.

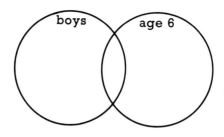

This can be used for up to three sets, allowing three intersections of two sets and one intersection of all three sets.

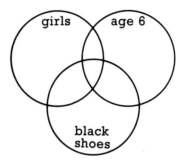

ACTIVITY 74   *Equipment*
the school registers

AT 5: 3a
Collect the school attendance numbers for each class, or for the school.

Use the information for graph work, and discuss:

- On which day were the most or the fewest children at school?
- Which class had the most children at school?
- Was the result the same each week?
- Was the result the same each day?

Discuss the reasons for the different figures, and for any fluctuations in the numbers.

ACTIVITY 75

Equipment
none

AT 5: 3b

Ask the children to consider school meals or packed lunches, and to decide on an element of the meal to investigate. They could look at the choice of potato dish (chips, baked, mashed) or flavour of crisps, or types of drinks in packed lunch boxes.

They need to design a data collection sheet, and ask a group of children what they have had for lunch that day. The information can then be recorded as a graph.

If more than one item in the meal is considered, they could use a Carroll diagram to record their findings.

ACTIVITY 76

Equipment
none

AT 5: 2b, 3c

Ask the children about things which will happen tomorrow, and discuss each suggestion they put forward. Ask questions such as:

- 'Why do you think that?'
- 'Are you sure?'
- 'Will that definitely happen?'

Ask other children for their opinions before accepting or rejecting a statement. This helps to develop confidence in their own thoughts and ideas, and encourages the skills of listening and evaluating.

They can be guided towards the right categorisation of each statement with extra suggestions such as:

- 'It will be Christmas Day tomorrow.'
- 'It will get dark tonight.'
- 'Tom will be 20 on his next birthday.'

- 'Tomorrow will be Sunday.'
- 'It will rain tomorrow.'

Ask them to consider whether each suggestion is **certain**, **uncertain** or **impossible**. Extra words can be helpful to bring the language within their understanding, such as:

- 'It **definitely** will happen.'
- 'It **might or might not** happen.'
- 'It **definitely** won't happen.'

AT 5: 3c The activity could be recorded in this form, using pictures drawn by the children to represent each suggestion that they have accepted for each category.

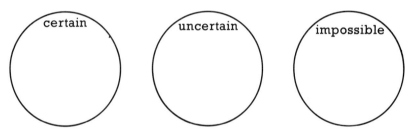

Alternatively, recording could make use of a simplified probability line, introducing children to the concept using information which they have already categorised. Again, ask them to draw a picture for each level of uncertainty.

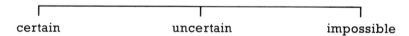

ACTIVITY 77

Equipment
two different objects (such as an apple and an orange)

AT 5: 1a Hide the objects behind your back, one in each hand. Ask the children in turn to choose left or right, and show them what is in that hand. Keep changing the objects from one hand to the other so that the outcome does not follow a regular pattern, and is random. As the children take their turn, ask them to record their outcome in picture form, then use the recordings to make a graph. They can use the graph to read and interpret the information obtained.

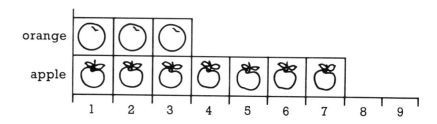

AT 5: 2a Talk about the results in the graph, and discuss

- the total number of events (10 in this case),
- the number of 'apple' outcomes,
- the number of 'orange' outcomes.
- $7 + 3 = 10$, $3 + 7 = 10$, $10 - 7 = 3$, $10 - 3 = 7$.

AT 2: 2a Look at the levels of the graph and compare the numbers. Count from 3 up to 7, and from 7 down to 3, to get the answer 4 in each case. Identify this as the 'difference'.

Discuss

> 3 oranges, 7 apples
> The difference is 4
> $7 - 3 = 4$

AT 1: 2c Talk about how the graph would change if you had an apple in each hand, giving only one possible outcome for each choice. Prompt the children to consider how the graph might change with three possible outcomes.

Vary the activity by using two socks, shapes or similar items, identical in all but colour, in an opaque bag. Ask children in turn to draw one out.